Under the Table and Screaming

fellini's

Miller's
Miller's
Live Music
LATE NIGHT FOOD
Full Menu
Featuring La COLOMBE
ABC ON & OFF LICENSED
Visit our THIRD FLOOR for SPORTS · CIGARS · BILLIARDS
Serving Charlottesville for More Than 35 Years
Miller's Downtown
KITCHEN OPEN UNTIL AM

Under the Table and

Screaming

Volume 2
Miller's
Fellini's No. 9

Erin O'Hare
Edited by Jay Mackenzie Baker

Charlottesville, Virginia

This work received the support of the UVA Arts Council, the UVA Vice Provost
for the Arts, and Virginia Humanities.

ARTS COUNCIL
UNIVERSITY of VIRGINIA

UNIVERSITY of VIRGINIA

**Virginia
Humanities**

LIBRARY OF CONGRESS CONTROL NUMBER: 2023917156

ISBN 979-8-9880587-2-4

Cover artwork by Thomas Dean.
All portraits by Sarah Everton.
Miller's introductory photo by Wikimedia Commons user Artaxerxes, CC BY-SA 4.0

We acknowledge the Monacan and Manahoac people, the traditional custodians of the unceded land of Charlottesville, where the events in this series take place and where this series was researched, reported, and written.

The title of this series is a reference to the Dave Matthews Band's debut full-length, *Under the Table and Dreaming*. A million and one pepperoni pizza slices worth of thanks to Alan Goffinski for coming up with it, and to everyone who laughed at it when WTJU General Manager Nathan Moore presented the options.

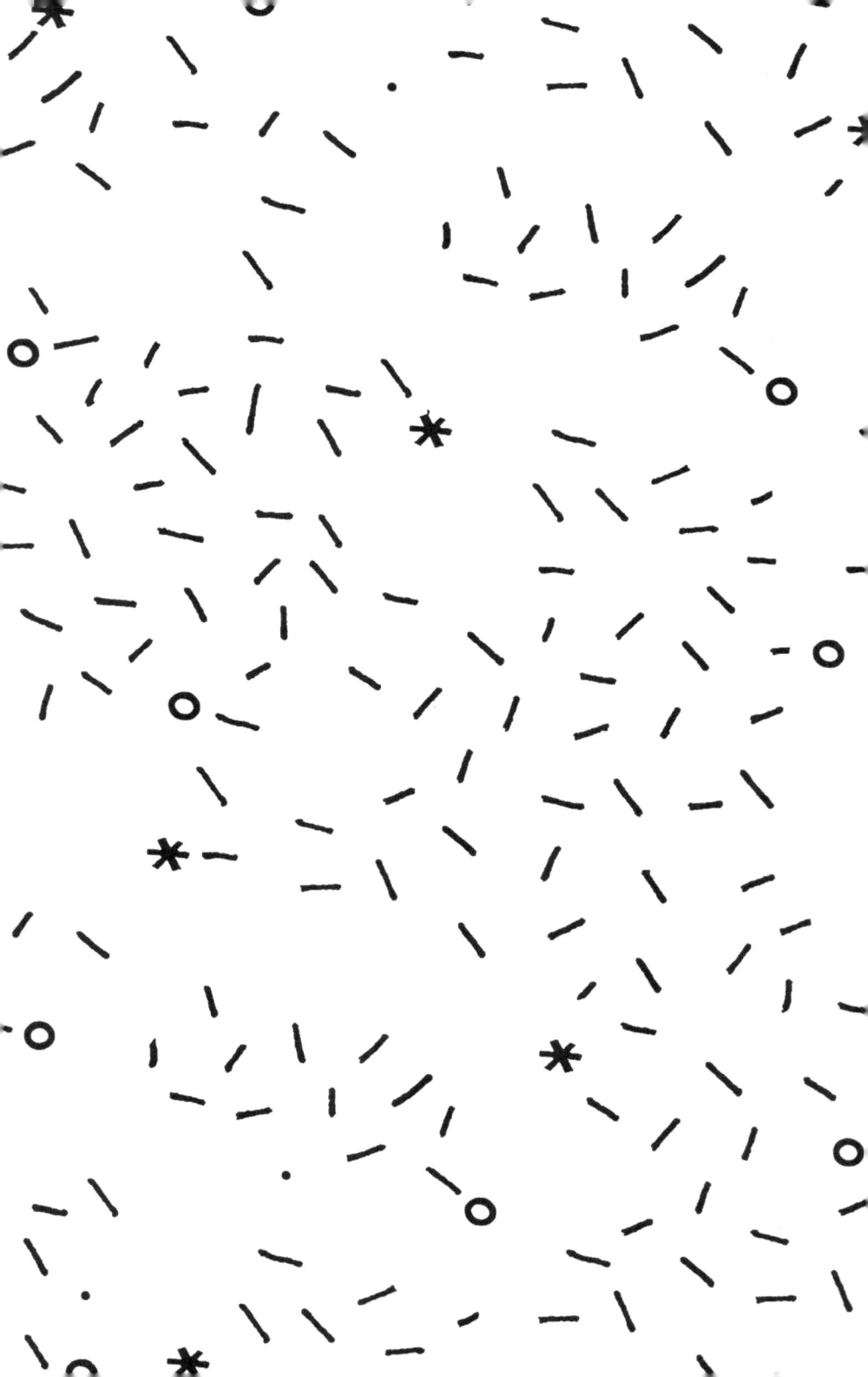

Contents

Note from WTJU

WTJU is more than just a radio station. I mean, it *is* a great radio station, serving UVA and the surrounding communities for nearly seven decades with classical, jazz, rock, folk, blues, world, r&b, hip-hop, and more. All hosted by your friends and neighbors who share your passion for music that moves you.

In Charlottesville's vibrant music ecosystem, WTJU is the fertile soil that nourishes. We bring people together through music and conversation, feeding a community that is curious, connected, and inclusive. Where there is music in Charlottesville, WTJU touches it.

What *does* it take to nourish a vibrant, independent music scene? It requires people who are passionate and committed. It requires people to run venues, bring people together, and create new sounds. In this zine series, you'll meet some of them. And just like we do on-air, WTJU will amplify their voices and enrich our culture. I'm so glad we can, and I'm glad you're along for the ride.

— Nathan Moore, WTJU General Manager

Why Under the Table?
Why Screaming?

Dave Matthews Band is by far the most famous musical act to emerge from Charlottesville (so far). Some folks cherish the local ties to DMB, whose titular frontman got his start as a bartender at Miller's downtown. Others are constantly trying to get out of the shadow the band casts in American popular music history.

Under the Table and Screaming gives a nod to that long shadow cast in the 1990s while delving into the people, places, and stories that keep our vibrant local music scene alive and thriving today. Because, despite DMB's success, they're not a quintessential Charlottesville band; there is no quintessential Charlottesville band, or even bands. There is no "Charlottesville sound." There are, in fact, a lot of sounds made in Charlottesville.

The music scene here isn't just dudes playing indie rock and jam bands for college kids (even if some of those jam bands really rock): It's the jazz legend who taught John Coltrane and Yusef Lateef and later lived, rather quietly, in Charlottesville. It's the female hardcore punk vocalist singing about feminism and identity in both English and Spanish. It's the teenager writing raps in his bedroom. It's the folk guitarist who's traveled the world.

Charlottesville's music culture is rich and varied, but discovering it takes some intentional effort. And the variety isn't necessarily what's touted by the venues that are part of the capital-M capital-B Music Business, which, in Charlottesville, mostly takes the form of Red Light Management, founded and owned by former DMB manager Coran Capshaw. The variety is instead found in restaurants and bars, in tea houses serving vegetarian food, in a house behind a massive magnolia tree. It's in the auditorium of an African American heritage center. It's in bedrooms and basements and backyards.

Some genres and artists have had to struggle for space more than others. And it's not easy. It takes decades of effort and an endless amount of heart. The work is always ongoing.

But if a town wants a local music scene, it must make the space for it. It must nourish it.

This series is about the ever-evolving group of people and places who've done that needful work, creating and keeping the flame of an independent local music culture. It's about those who have championed music made by and for the people who live here. And it's about the many ways to keep that music alive: start a band, bring your friend's band to town, set up a show, make posters, write about local acts, pay for a ticket, or buy some merch. Go to a show and maybe even dance around a little.

Under the Table and Screaming is about a local music scene. Every place has one, and this one is ours.

Under the Table

and Screaming

MILLER'S

Miller's is a bar, restaurant, and community hub for live music (especially jazz) that has been in continuous operation for over four decades. It hosts regular gigs on Wednesdays and Thursdays, both running for nearly as long as Miller's itself, with plenty of other shows in between. With three floors, each offering a different experience, Miller's is a staple of the Downtown Mall, located at 109 West Main Street, one of the Mall's oldest buildings. Placed near entertainment attractions like Violet Crown, The Jefferson Theater, and The Paramount Theater, Miller's welcomes late-night mallcrawlers galore for some of the best music you'll find anywhere in town.

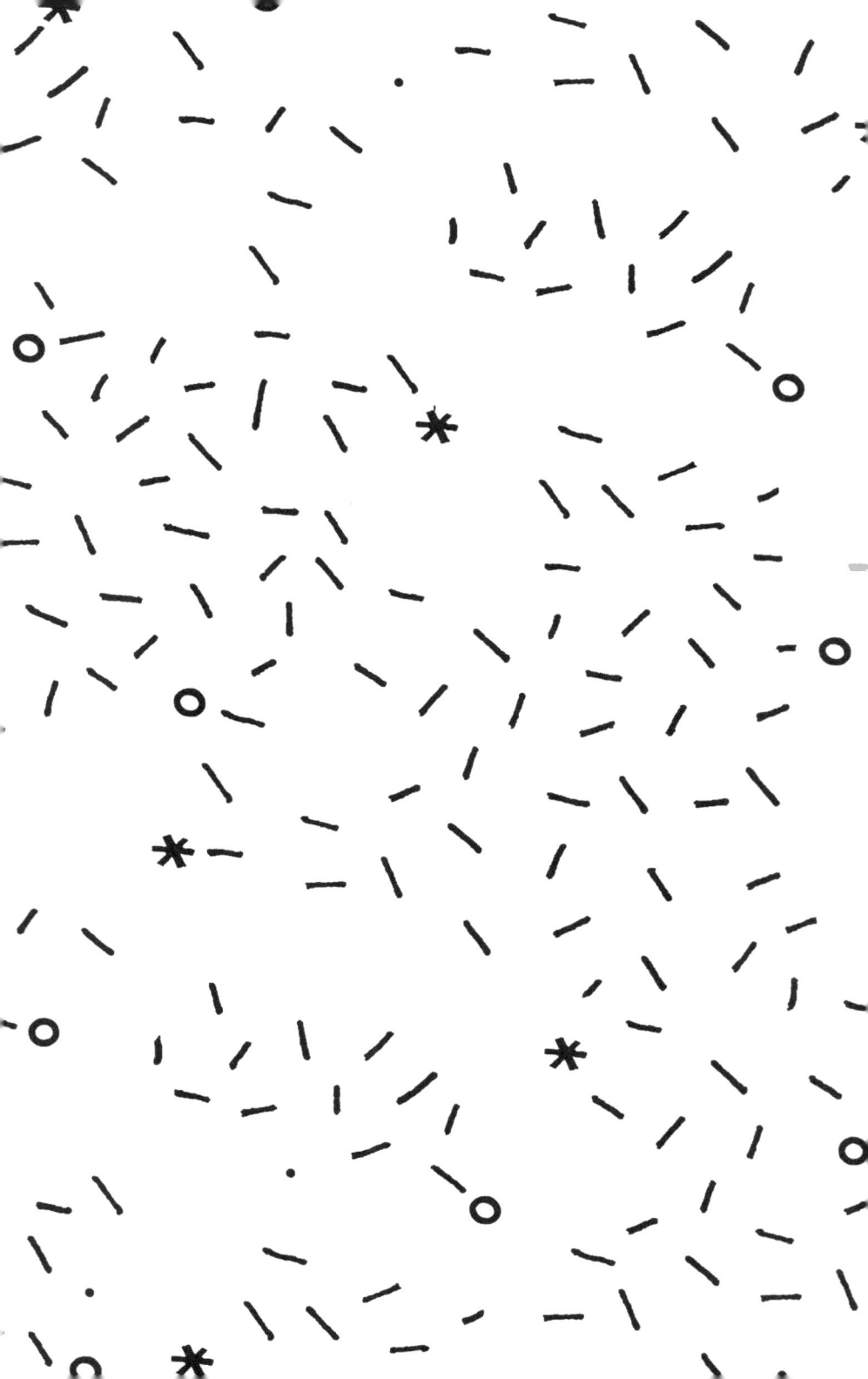

"No Place Like Miller's"

The History of a Charlottesville Music Pillar

One weekend in the mid-to-late '70s, New York City jazz-rock fusion band Cosmology drove down to Charlottesville for a gig in the Hunt Room at the Monticello Hotel.[†]

Cosmology had some history in town: founder and bassist Reed Wasson attended law school at UVA in the 1960s before returning to his hometown of New York City, where he met his bandmates (and played with many other upper-level jazz musicians). Wasson had brought Cosmology down to Charlottesville for a few gigs before this one, but this Monticello Hotel show was their first gig in the area with someone as well-known as avant-garde jazz guitarist John Abercrombie, whose bright star was on the rise at the time.

> **THE HUNT ROOM –**
>
> A social room in the Monticello Hotel, located in Court Square in Downtown Charlottesville. The hotel opened in the 1920s, and sometimes had music in the Hunt Room. In the mid-1970s, the hotel was converted to condominiums.

> **COSMOLOGY –**
>
> Jazz-rock fusion band co-founded in the 1970s by John D'earth, Robert Jospé and Dawn Thompson. The band released a self-titled album on the revered Vanguard Records label in 1977.

But whoever booked the gig must have been unfamiliar with the venue, the band, or both, says Cosmology trumpet player John D'earth: With a seven-piece band and no stage, there would have been space for a dozen audience members in the Hunt Room at best.

The Sitting Ducks, a local group that played mostly early swing music with some jazz flavor, heard about Cosmology's problem and offered to stand down their own gig at the Stacks, a venue in the downstairs of the Library Restaurant, to give Cosmology a room spacious enough for the audience Abercrombie would draw.

Pete Spaar, Sitting Ducks' bass player, doesn't quite remember why his band opted to hand its gig over to Cosmology that night. The details are a bit fuzzy: it was the '70s after all. Maybe the gig didn't pay well, or maybe Sitting Ducks was double-booked. But Spaar prefers "to think it was because of our magnanimity and selfless love for the music scene in Charlottesville."

John D'earth, a hard bop and post-bop trumpet player who has recorded a number of his own albums and appeared on records by Bruce Hornsby and the Dave Matthews Band. D'earth has led Thursday night jazz at Miller's for decades. He also teaches jazz performance at the University of Virginia and plays in the faculty ensemble, the Free Bridge Quintet.

Pete Spaar, a classical and jazz bassist. Spaar has been principal bassist of the Charlottesville Symphony since 1993. He also teaches performance at the University of Virginia, and plays Thursday nights at Miller's, and in the Free Bridge Quintet, among other groups.

Lines formed around the block from the Stacks. D'earth remembers "We had to do two shows in a night and clear the room, because the guy playing with us [Abercrombie] was so famous in jazz guitar, and his career was at its peak … he was playing with a lot of heavyweight people. He had his own band, he was on ECM Records, and he was just a real artist, a real voice."

A band handing its gig over to another group would never have happened in New York, says D'earth. To him, that story is the epitome of Charlottesville. "That's Charlottesville. We were so welcomed."

Before long, D'earth moved from New York to Charlottesville, in the summer of 1981. His arrival just so happened to coincide with the opening of Charlottesville's longest-running music spot, a would-be jazz club (were it not for strict ABC laws) whose reputation extends far beyond Central Virginia. A restaurant-bar whose four decades of continuous operation have probably begat as many stories as pints of beer poured. Some of those stories have been heard around the world. Most of them resonate somewhere closer, at home in the hearts and minds of local musicians and music fans past and present.

A Music Magnet Despite All Odds

Steve Tharp opened Miller's in the old Miller Drugstore on the Downtown Mall in August of 1981. The former occupant's painted sign—*Miller Drug-Store: Drugs, Seeds*—remains, faded on the building's brick façade and visible above the green awning that bears the restaurant-bar's name in white script. Inside, the place feels like an old-school neighborhood joint: dark wood, dim lights, and a bar that maintains a sort of apothecary soda fountain feel. Near the front, visible through the mallside windows on the first floor, is a stage for music.

Music "was always part of the game plan," says Tharp, who was inspired to open a jazz club in part by his years working in the kitchen of the Gaslight Restaurant on West Main Street.[†]

The Gaslight's kitchen was pure chaos most of the time, "crazy and loud and noisy," says Tharp. But whenever he'd walk out into the dining room, it was, by contrast, "dimly lit—candlelit—quiet, [with] people murmuring and glassware tinkling and this jazz trio playing. It was like magic. It was a whole different world. It was mystical."

> GASLIGHT RESTAURANT –
> Opened in the early 1960s, this restaurant-bar occupied a few different spots on the 600 block of West Main Street (across the street from the Amtrak train station). A slew of local musicians played there, and a few big names —Bob Dylan, Joan Baez—reportedly played there, too. It closed sometime between 1993 and 1995.

Steve Tharp, founder of Miller's.

That enchanting atmosphere only reinforced Tharp's longtime fantasy of running his own jazz club. But Virginia's ABC laws were (and still are) extraordinarily strict, and made it virtually impossible to have one anywhere in the Commonwealth. By Tharp's recollection, Miller's, like other spots, had to be able to prove to the ABC officers who stopped by to check the books that at least half of its income came from food. If more than half came from alcohol sales, the officer could pull the liquor license.

Below: Miller's, looking in from the entryway. The stage, with its wraparound windows, is to the right. Photo courtesy of Eze Amos.

Still, Tharp thought Charlottesville—with its appetite for music and other art forms—could both use and support a place like Miller's. So he gave it a go and booked whomever he could get to come in. In those early days, before Miller's established itself as a Charlottesville jazz mainstay, the music atmosphere felt somewhat like a coffeehouse. At first, there was live music two or three nights a week. Acts like country-folk singer-songwriters Terri Allard and Billy Brockman played often, as well as other traditional and roots musicians from around town.

Things really got going music-wise for Miller's when John D'earth and two of his Cosmology bandmates, singer Dawn Thompson (D'earth's wife) and percussionist Robert Jospé, started playing jazz gigs at Miller's in various combinations. The early Miller's scene was helped along when the C&O restaurant eventually stopped hosting jazz, leading that crowd to migrate a few blocks down to Miller's.[†]

By the mid-1980s—or maybe it was the late 1980s … no one knows exactly when—D'earth, Thompson, and Jospé started playing a regular Thursday night gig. Tharp credits that jazz gig with helping Miller's change gears: more people started coming in, and more groups wanted to play regular gigs—jazz gigs. It felt less like a coffeehouse (not that there's any-

> **C&O –**
> Located at 515 E. Water St., Philip Stafford and Sandy Adams (also of Daedalus Books on Fourth St.) opened this restaurant-bar in 1976. At one point, they regularly hosted jazz and blues music, and tried punk once (just the once). There's usually a record on in the bar part of the building, which was built with wood from an old barn in Crozet.

thing wrong with a coffeehouse) and more like a jazz club, says Tharp, who at that point felt like he'd finally realized his dream. Eventually, Miller's came to have music just about every night of the week.

But that didn't mean things were easy. Both the music and restaurant businesses are unpredictable; many bands will fizzle out after a few months or years, and the same goes for many restaurants, even successful ones.

"What made it possible for me was that these guys would play just out of their generosity, their craft. They wanted a place to play, for someone to give them a forum," says Tharp. In many cases, the artists Miller's has hosted throughout the years are by and large extraordinarily talented "and should have been well-compensated, but we just didn't have the money. We couldn't afford it," he adds, noting that most artists played for tips. Eventually, the bar tried a cover charge for a while. But in Tharp's opinion, the musicians never made close to what they deserved, particularly because they really were (and still are) top-drawer players.

"People passing through town would always be shocked at the level of music they heard at Miller's," says Spaar. "People from New York would go, 'oh my god, what are you doing in a little town like this?' Because it became a magnet for the best musicianship around. [That] high level of musicianship there … was appreciated by a good chunk of the audience, but [it] didn't really matter to probably the majority of [them]. Somehow that all coexisted."

What's more, downtown Charlottesville wasn't yet the locus of entertainment that it is today.

"I'll be really honest and say, it was an air of adventure and danger in the late '80s and early '90s, going gigging downtown," says multi-instrumentalist Ivan Orr, who was a student at Charlottesville High School at the time. Orr, a member of both the CHS pep band and the original go-go act Ebony Groove, occasionally played Miller's with Ian Gordon, one of D'earth's first local students. Gordon, appropriately enough, is the son of the couple who started Fellini's, another longtime reliable local spot for live jazz, just around the corner from Miller's.

"It was kind of like a ghost town, nobody [around]," says Orr about the downtown area at the time. "It felt more like weirdo Charlottesvillian at that point, as opposed to a transplants, tourists kind of thing" that it is now.

But the music has always been superb. The first night Orr played saxophone with Gordon at Miller's, they had legendary local musicians behind them: Johnny Gilmore on drums and (probably, though Orr's not positive) Houston Ross on bass. "I don't even know if we had anyone playing piano or guitar," Orr recalls, "just horns, bass, and drums." He suspects his and Gordon's youth compelled their listeners to fill the tip jar, but with such an expert rhythm section on stage, who's really to say?

The Miller's stage is often filled with world-class musicians who draw crowds in big city jazz clubs. And yet, on any given night, most people aren't there for the music. There's no fanfare or announcement, no "… and now …!" before the music begins. The band starts when it's ready, and those there for the music know what they're in for. Others seem surprised that there's music happening at all.

Many in the audience don't know that it's where local music legends, including saxophonist LeRoi Moore and drummer Johnny Gilmore (who played together in a group called Soko) played. That it's where nationally-acclaimed artists, like acoustic blues and reggae guitarist (and 2007 MacArthur Genius Grant winner) Corey Harris and the late Emily Remler, who's been called "a forgotten giant of jazz guitar" by *Jazz Times*, played regular gigs. That it's where artists like Houston Ross and John D'earth and Devonne Harris (of Butcher Brown) continue to play. That it's where the founding members of Dave Matthews Band, including Matthews himself, met and formed their world-famous band.

"The atmosphere of Miller's, in a lot of ways, is not pious," says D'earth. "It's not reverential to the music at all, which annoys some musicians, but to me, it doesn't. I say we're all allowed to be in here, and if people want to yell and listen and scream while we're playing, that's their loss, and also people can come up front to listen. That has kind of worked itself out in a natural way."[†]

Ivan Orr. As a teenager, he was a member of the Charlottesville High School pep band and the original go-go act Ebony Groove. In addition to playing music in churches, he's composed for a variety of projects, including the documentary "Raised/Razed," which aired nationally in 2022 and is available online, about the destruction of Vinegar Hill, one of Charlottesville's oldest majority Black neighborhoods.

But sometimes the talkers are right up front, and that's hard on the artists. D'earth admits to losing his cool every now and then and chewing out the occasional up-front loud-talker or band-heckler from the bandstand (and usually apologizing after the fact).

Despite generally embracing its noise and light chaos, Miller's doesn't tolerate jackasses. Plenty of folks have been kicked out for life for unsavory behavior (though some have made their way back in

> LISTENING THROUGH THE NOISE –
>
> Miller's music regulars know that the best music experience is at a table up close to the bandstand, where they don't have to strain to hear the notes over the din of loud bar conversations about shitty bosses, bridezillas, and breakups, where they can say hello to the musicians between set breaks. Though acoustically speaking, the best listening spot in the room is all the way at the back, against the wall near the first-floor bathrooms and the stairs to the second floor.

after enough time has passed and staff has turned over). And in summer 2017, when neo-Nazis and other white supremacist groups showed up in town over and over again, D'earth made sure to put a sign in the Miller's window during his Thursday night gigs to let everyone know that the music that he and his band were playing—jazz—is their reverent interpretation of Black music.

The chaos inside Miller's is a warm one. It's the sound of a community, and community is loud. "It was like a sitcom in a way," recalls country-ish singer-songwriter Sarah White of her time there in the 1990s and 2000s. Throughout high school and college, White and her friends would go there to drink coffee (and eventually alcohol), smoke cigarettes, "and try to be deep," she says.

Performing solo and with her various bands, and at one point even working in the kitchen, mostly making nachos, White saw the warmth of Miller's up-close: "It's hard to know, sometimes, if you're looking at it through the lens of youthful hopefulness. There was drama, there were characters, there were really good friendships. There were fights. There was music.

Playing the Changes, and More of the Same

The Miller's entryway. Stairs to upper floors are behind the left windows, with the stage just out of view on the right. Photo courtesy of Eze Amos.

All businesses, all scenes, change over time. Despite its throwback vibe, Miller's isn't immune. Miller's has always been a little rough around the edges, though those edges have worn down a bit over the years as Charlottesville itself has become a little glossier, putting tourism and certain kinds of business before art.

Tharp sold the business in 2001, and some folks say that while its charm remains, the place has felt shinier and less lived-in ever since. The old pharmacy storefront is gone. The third floor, where Tharp lived, is now a pool hall of sorts. The bar, which initially extended all the way to the front windows, is smaller. And, in order to fit more seating, the stage keeps shrinking, much to the musicians' chagrin.

It's tough to fit a band and its clunky gear on the little elevated platform in the front window, right inside the door, but most players have a sense of humor about this particular quirk, comparing it to a fishbowl: It tends to get a little damp, and there are always people peering in to see what they're doing. Some artists like it more than others—it makes blues-ish electric guitarist Jamal Millner feel like he's "in a zoo or something," and messes with his concentration. Singer Richelle Claiborne, who says she is "the exhibitionist, not the voyeur," loves performing in the window, where she can usually lure someone in from outside for the remainder of the set.

"It's kinda cramped," says Spaar, who usually finds himself and his upright bass all the way in the back corner with the drummer, with the horns up front. "Different bands use different arrangements, but you have to be resourceful, depending on the size of the band."

At one point, there was a dead rat (they're pretty sure it was a dead rat) under the stage, and it stank to high heaven as the night went on and the room warmed up. Long ago, someone spilled a big jug of Coke syrup (at least, they hope it's Coke syrup) on the second floor, and on especially hot nights it drips sticky-thick through the pressed tin ceiling tiles and into the musicians' hair. It's surprisingly difficult to wash out.

For many years, patrons could smoke cigarettes (but not cloves or cigars) inside, and a cinematic blue-gray haze hung in the air. Every now and then, someone would forget a lit cigarette in an ashtray and cause a small fire. Musicians would come home smelling like butts even if they didn't smoke, and some joke that if they ever get lung cancer, it'll be because of Miller's. That changed in 2009, though, and anyone who wants to have a smoke while enjoying the band has to step outside and hear a muffled version of the set from the other side of the fishbowl window.

But certain things about Miller's have long remained the same: Namely, the diverse crowd that includes longtime locals, UVA students, street kids, punks, tourists coming in off the mall, and Dave Matthews Band superfans. It's drawn in Kennedys (yes, *those* Kennedys, as some of them went to UVA) and famous playwrights (including Sam Shepard, who was reportedly banned for picking a fight with a popular local musician). It's drawn people from different cultures, socioeconomic classes, and groups who might not otherwise mingle (Richelle Claiborne is convinced this occurs in large part because Miller's has the best steaks in town).

"Everyone was in there, everyone was welcome," says Jamal Millner, who started going to Miller's for jazz when he was a UVA student in the late 1980s and early 1990s. "We talk about how [Charlottesville] is segregated, it really is, but Miller's was one of those spots that was not," says Millner. "It'd be millionaires, bikers, white supremacists, Black gang members, just all in there at the same time, chillin'. And everything in-between, regular people, whatever." While other venues, like the Outback Lodge and The Ante Room, once boasted similarly eclectic crowds, Miller's outlasted them both.[†]

Jamal Millner. Millner landed in Charlottesville from a small town in West Virginia on a scholarship to UVA. He spent years as a professional guitarist, most notably in the electric blues/ reggae band Corey Harris & The 5x5, before taking a pro sound production gig with Virginia Humanities. He's also played with Vusi Mahlasela, Buddy Guy, R.L. Burnside, Ali Farka Toure, and the Dave Matthews Band.

In every era, Miller's has been full of characters, like Ed Waxman, "the natural music man," a regular from way back when. Waxman used to sit in the back of Miller's, smoking a pipe and saying "oh, yeah yeah! Oh, yeah yeah!" He played guitar too, and wrote songs about love and soup bowls that Sarah White remembers as being "so fucking deep and yet also just so insane." Another regular, Sidney, used to hop on stage on a whim and play harmonica with the bands if he was digging what he heard.

THE ANTE ROOM –

The Ante Room operated from 2012 to 2018. It was originally called The Annex before being re-named. At the west end of the Downtown Mall facing Water Street, it shared a roof with an ice arena and the gay bar/restaurant Escafé. The building holding all three spots—and the cultures they supported—was demolished to build the CODE building, a co-working and think tank space.

OUTBACK LODGE –
Terry Martin opened the Outback Lodge in 1992 at 917 Preston Avenue. It hosted everything from hip-hop to street punk and even goth night for a while. It closed in 2010.

And of course, the staff, many of whom spend years working at Miller's and getting to know the musicians and regulars, are a big part of keeping the hip vibe alive.

Yet the most obvious constant has been the music. When Tharp sold Miller's, the next (and current) owners, Dedra and Scottie Taylor, let all the musicians keep their gigs, which is a rarity in the music and restaurant worlds. But in many ways, both philosophical and economical, music is the backbone of Miller's. It wouldn't be the same establishment if the music didn't continue uninterrupted by the change in ownership. For many folks, Miller's is at the heart of the local music scene, and the constant presence of music there has been vital to genres even beyond jazz.

It's Not Just Great Jazz

For a while, there was a strong avant-garde presence at Miller's. Greg Howard would play nights on the Chapman Stick, an instrument that looks like an extra-wide guitar neck with 10 or 12 individually tuned strings used to play melodies, chords, bass lines, and more.

Tim Reynolds' had the regular Monday night show at Miller's for a while, and he was allowed to play whatever he wanted. He had the chops, and Mondays were a bit slow, so it's not like he could scare anyone away, jokes Tharp. Reynolds is by all accounts a "monster" of a guitar player, as well as a multi-instrumentalist; for some gigs, he'd show up with a violin, or a sitar instead of his guitar, or add his own bonkers spin on a well-known tune.

Reynolds' Monday night sets were particularly memorable for guitarist Jamal Millner, who has played in various groups in town since the late 1980s, including on Thursdays with John D'earth. Millner would ride his bike from his home on Cabell Avenue to Miller's to hear Reynolds play, whether solo or with his group The Mutants, consisting of Reynolds on guitar, Johnny Gilmore on drums, and either Houston Ross or Pete Spaar on bass.

Millner's bike ride to Miller's was almost entirely downhill, but in the other direction—after a night of ingesting mind-blowing music and maybe a drink or two—he had an uphill pedal home through the wee hours of the morning, hoping to catch a couple hours' sleep before his morning classes.

But oh, was it worth it, he says, to feel like he was in the Village in New York City. Reynolds "would play crazy music, like, atonal, crazy, free jazz.

[…] If you just walked into Miller's in 1993 or something, you could have been in New York."

Like the night Reynolds, Ross, and Gilmore played one of Reynolds' concoctions, "Stairway to Green Acres," which Millner says is "the best, my funniest memory ever." For comparison, Millner offers American composer Charles Ives' tendency to play more than one kind of music at a time, with one part of an orchestra playing one composition while a second group of the orchestra played something different. "He wanted it to sound like you're at a parade, and you can hear one band showing up and another one leaving, and you're in the spot where you can hear them both," says Millner. This one night at Miller's, the rhythm section—Ross and Gilmore—played the "Green Acres" theme as a groove while Reynolds played "Stairway to Heaven" in its entirety, simultaneously.

Upon hearing this, a guy in the audience freaked, and "started tripping," says Millner. The man got up on stage and backed Reynolds into one of the little cutouts at the back of the old stage. The band didn't miss a note as this was happening. Gilmore stood up, his foot still going on the kick drum pedal, da-da-da-da-da-da-da-da. Without skipping a beat, he yelled at the guy, "get the fuck off the stage!"

The tripper indeed got the fuck off the stage and the band continued its set. "That shit was amazing," says Millner, laughing. It was as if it was planned—that's how well the band handled it all. "That kind of stuff would happen at Miller's *all the time*."

Brennan Gilmore also frequently played Miller's with his bluegrass/ newgrass band, Walker's Run, in the early 2000s. "We had tons of amazing nights at Miller's, a bunch of college kids standing up on the tables flat-footing to fiddle tunes, stuff like that." But his favorite Miller's music memory isn't so much about the music itself as it is the kind of odd situations people can find themselves in as a result of it. Gilmore's music-loving parents would drive to Charlottesville from Lexington to see Walker's Run play and they'd always bring Gilmore's kid sister along, who was 10 or 11 at the time. One (late) night, his sister fell asleep in the front window, and a few cops came through the door and mid-song told the band and staff that a kid couldn't be sleeping in the window of a bar. Gilmore cracks up when he remembers the story, and his parents' reaction of "Oh, she just came to see her brother play music." Bluegrass music is pretty family-friendly anyway, says Gilmore, who's had friends sneak their babies in under trench coats.

Friday and Saturday nights are typically reserved for touring bands (like rock acts Thao and the Get Down Stay Down and The Steel Wheels, both of whom played Miller's before getting big), or for local groups that don't have regular gigs. These weekend shows let Miller's mix the calendar up a bit and get a few new folks in the door each time. There's a different kind of spontaneity that can only result from one-off gigs. Like the time Tharp was behind the bar, listening to a solo pianist play on the (now long-gone) in-house piano while he poured drinks and put food orders through to the kitchen. A guy walked toward the pianist, picked a couple knives off a nearby table, and started playing percussion on the little tin lamp illuminating the piano. Tharp watched closely, anticipating having to toss this (potentially drunk) guy out of the place if he started heckling the pianist. But then he noticed the pianist was into it, and that the guy was actually pretty good. When Tharp got a closer look, he recognized the knife-drummer: Robert Jospé, member of Cosmology and, for a long time, D'earth's Thursday night drummer.

The unpredictability of the weekend nights is usually the result of an increasingly inebriated audience, not the music. Gina Sobel, a young multi-instrumentalist and singer whose music bridges many genres, from jazz to funk to Sephardic fusion and many spaces in-between, has played those gigs with her bands, including Choose Your Own Adventure and The Mighty Fine. One night, someone stole their tip jar during the set break. The audience was so pissed that someone would do that, they filled the jar again—and then some—by the end of the night. Another weekend, someone ran up to the bandstand and threw 100 one-dollar bills at the band.

A Tale of Two Gigs

Miller's stands out among other Charlottesville venues—among most any venue, anywhere—in that it's hosted two of the longest-running regular jazz gigs in the region (perhaps even in the country). Gigs paused only for the COVID-19 pandemic shutdown.

On Wednesday nights, saxophonist Jeff Decker, guitarist Mike Rosensky and their quartet have played since the mid-1990s. And going back even further, John D'earth has played nearly every Thursday with some combination of musicians since the late 1980s. Nobody knows exactly when, but D'earth estimates it was after 1986.

These two weekly gigs share a venue and sometimes musicians as well as a taste for modern jazz and post-bop. Otherwise, they're quite different, each a testament to how music can influence and even overtake the atmosphere in a place.

On Wednesday nights, the music starts around 9:30. The group plays two sets of originals, modern jazz standards, and occasionally, interpretations of popular songs. Every week it's a different set—an impressive feat considering the gig's longevity.

"They come in early, stop early, and just do what they do quietly, beautifully," says Cathy Monnes, an experimental cellist who dabbles in a variety of genres and who frequents Miller's gigs, having played in a number of them herself over the years.

Jeff Decker. Primarily a saxophonist, he's played with various groups in town, including Robert Jospé's Inner Rhythm and the Free Bridge Quintet. He holds down Wednesday night jazz with Mike Rosensky, and has also taught performance at UVA and Piedmont Virginia Community College.

"Some people might say Wednesdays are slower" than Thursdays, says Decker, "but they're really just more subdued" due in part to the start and end time and in part to the day of the week. According to Decker, they get a lot of folks streaming in for a nightcap after a movie or after a more raucous show at The Jefferson Theater or The Paramount.

The Wednesday night band keeps it fresh by updating their repertoire often, and by tying the set into what's happening in music news. When actress Ja'Net DuBois, who played Willona Woods on the television show *Good Times* and subsequently wrote and sang "Movin' On Up," the theme song for *Good Times* spinoff *The Jeffersons,* died in February 2020, Decker wanted to honor her with a rendition of her famous tune. When rock 'n' roll pioneer Fats Domino died in October 2017, they played a set in his honor, including Domino's hit rendition of "Blueberry Hill." A jazz group playing Fats Domino tunes might surprise some people, says Decker, "but that's one of the beauties of jazz. We can figure out a way." It helps, says Decker, that after so many years of playing together in a tight-knit group, they know one another's playing styles, strengths, and limitations quite well.

But while the musicians try to treat their audience to something new every week, sometimes the musicians are the ones being surprised.

One Wednesday night a few years back, in the mid-2010s, the quartet was playing a tune called "Passion Dance" by McCoy Tyner. During the saxophone solo, Decker closed his eyes, as he often does, in order to completely lose himself in the music. When he played the last note of the solo, though, he still heard … saxophone? He opened his eyes, followed the sound to his left and saw a college classmate (they graduated in 1987) standing there blaring out the notes on an alto sax. Turns out Decker's former classmate was on tour with Lyle Lovett, who'd just played a show at the Charlottesville Pavilion and had looked around to see if Decker happened to be playing a set of his own that night. The two former music school classmates battled, trading lines and phrases on their saxophones as if they were back in college, just starting their lifelong journeys in jazz.

For his part, guitarist Rosensky feels fortunate to have a gig like this, adding that it's gone on for so long "because we like to play."

As for the other long-running Miller's jazz gig, John D'earth says half-jokingly that there must be something wrong with him to have kept Thursday nights going for more than 30 years. He's cycled through a few different groups of musicians in that time as people come to town and move away, burn out on the gig, or just want to do something different.

At first, music started at 9:30 on Thursday nights, just like on Wednesdays. But its informal nature meant that after a while, the musicians started showing up at 9:30 and got the music going by 10 o'clock. Then it became a 10:15 start, then 10:30, and lately, they're lucky if the music gets going by 11 (and the music starts, by the way, when D'earth arrives.) "That sort of sets the tone," says Spaar. "It's a very laid-back gig in that regard, but everybody is very dedicated. And the way it's worked, it's always a sort of core group of musicians, but a huge community of musicians revolving around that core, and musicians coming from all over—Richmond, Washington, D.C.," and sometimes further.

D'earth is usually loath to stop at 2am, sometimes going until 2:30, or even 3 if he can push it.

"It's just *absolutely* insane," says Charles Owens, who's played everywhere from Richmond to New York City to Miami to Chicago, and who plays Miller's regularly, sometimes with D'earth's group, or holding Thursday nights down himself if D'earth can't make it. "No gigs last that long. No gigs last half that long. Seriously. I'm not exaggerating."

Thursday nights are always packed and usually devolve into a jam session of sorts. D'earth almost always plays with Pete Spaar on bass and usually has Devonne Harris of Butcher Brown fame on drums (though a rotating cast of drummers have made appearances in recent years). He's always inviting other master musicians or his star students (he teaches private lessons and at UVA) to sit in with them too, so it's more or less a different lineup every week. D'earth wouldn't be surprised if the list of people who've sat in with him at Miller's, from those early Cosmology sets to the Thursday night gigs, reaches into the hundreds. The music is always evolving, too, depending on who's in the band. When Millner was playing with the Thursday night group, for example, he brought a bit of the blues and some Afro vibes to the set.

Miller's on a Thursday night. John D'earth (trumpet, center) has brought in many different musicians over the years. This night happened to include Butch Taylor (piano), JC Kuhl (saxophone, back turned), and Pete Spaar (bass, back left, "without whom nothing"). Photo by Dee Claudio Zarpelon, courtesy of Gina Sobel.

And it's a scene unto itself. With a batch of devotees who come every week, or most weeks, hanging around until the last note fades, always going back on the promises they make to themselves not to stay out too late.

That devoted audience is just as important as the music in a way, says Dhara Goradia, a bassist who's played Miller's since the mid-2000s. She sometimes subs in when Spaar can't make the gig and frequently goes just to listen and watch. "You're not just sitting there watching a concert," says Goradia. "You're there to be part of the scene."

These gigs are "really high-energy," adds Goradia. "Incredible levels of playing, really, the most creative group of musicians in one spot, and people who are willing to try new things at every moment, and John rallying everyone around him and just generating this really intoxicating energy around him. […] The energy there is really unmatched. [Miller's is] the only place in town that gives you that kind of outlet, I would say, that sort of freedom and a high level of playing in the same place."

Praise for the Thursday night gig is high and plentiful. "A singular experience," says Gary Funston, co-founder of the Charlottesville Jazz Society and longtime WTJU jazz DJ. "To me, that's a real jazz club experience, packed in tightly, they're on that tiny stage."

"They have held church there, those guys. The John D'earth Thursday night thing has been church," says cellist Monnes. Those Thursday night gigs are indeed a ritual, a creative communion for many.

It's just as meaningful to those on the stage. "Playing with John is great because it's very inspiring," says Owens. "I'm only as good as the people I play with, because I like to listen very closely to the people I play with. When John plays, it's really inspiring for me to dig deeper within myself to really try to convey a sincerity in my emotional content, confidence, clarity. Playing with him is hallowed ground. It's rarefied air."

"Those gigs are special and beautiful, and also, the community down there of the people who come every week—not just the patrons, but the musicians who come and sit in every week—to play this music," Owens adds. "It's vital that people have a place to come and try shit out, and experiment, because that's what improvisational music is, the spirit happening right in front of everyone. We're sound scientists, and we need to experiment with people. We need the real world to do it. We can only do so much in our practice room," says Owens. He also loves how he can play his saxophone as loud as he wants at Miller's and nobody ever tells him to pipe down.

Spaar also uses the same scientific language of experimentation to describe Thursday nights at Miller's, comparing Miller's to a laboratory—a place where they can try out new things and take risks in ways they can't in other venues.

"These are the kinds of gigs that pro players in big cities would kill for," says Spaar. "I don't know where I would be as a musician if I didn't have this steady Thursday night gig at Miller's to explore and develop and grow,

[to] play with different musicians but always at a high level. It's been the equivalent of having a school of music for me, a lab where you can go and try things out. […] My friends who gravitated to New York and play up there are envious! They will travel an hour and a half on the subway from Brooklyn to Manhattan to play, schlepping their bass on whatever line, or taking a cab, to get to a gig that pays $50, so they end up losing money on the night, if they can even get the gig. And they're happy to get the gig. And here I've got a gig of that level that I can drive to [and] park for free (I'm really good at finding downtown parking—because I have to lug my bass)."

Spaar, D'earth, and the others can do all this while wearing their jeans and flannel shirts to boot. They, as well as plenty of other folks who play Miller's—Rosensky and Decker included—teach in the music department at UVA, where they don tuxedos to play a number of more formal and rehearsed shows at Old Cabell Hall.

For these reasons, D'earth even views the two venues as opposite sides of the same coin. And indeed, part of the appeal of going to those gigs at Miller's as a UVA student, per bluegrass musician Brennan Gilmore, is getting the chance to see one's professors play the flipside of that coin, outside of

the university setting. Gilmore took D'earth's jazz improv class in Old Cabell Hall when he was a student at UVA, and he and his friends would often go to Miller's on Thursday nights. That was "another one of those cool aspects of being in Charlottesville […], playing with and living among and watching your musical heroes, no walls between."

Miller's has had some spectacular guests over the years. Pictured above is Stevie Wonder, surrounded by Miller's patrons and staff. Photo courtesy of Jess Martin.

A Memorable Episode

At one point, D'earth realized that the music just got better and better every week. He was consistently having his mind blown by his regular bandmates and by the folks sitting in. "Every week, year in and year out, I would be like, 'I can't believe what happened at Miller's! Oh my god!'" he says. The music is so consistently great that it's usually the not-so-great nights that stick out to him.

But there's one good music night that D'Earth will never forget: the night that Pureum Jin walked in.

Jin, a saxophonist, was born in South Korea and steeped in the blues. She moved to Charlottesville from New York with her husband, who'd landed a job in town, and some of her city jazz pals told her she had to meet John D'earth. Jin did a little research and saw that D'earth and his band played Miller's every Thursday. So she went to see if she could sit in and play with them.

Jin's pretty sure it was late July 2017 when she first walked through the front door of Miller's on a Thursday night. "The bar was filled with people and jazz was everywhere, and there were almost 10 horn players close to the stage," Jin remembers. She was three months pregnant with her first child and had her saxophone case slung over her shoulder.

It was a pro-quality case: it caught the eye of D'earth and a few others who knew there must be a pretty sweet instrument inside to warrant that kind of protection. When Jin introduced herself and asked to sit in, D'earth (who guards the proverbial gate to the bandstand

Pureum Jin, a bright star in the global jazz sky. Pureum Jin is a saxophonist and composer based in New York City. Born in Seoul, Korea, her name translates to "The Real Blue" in English. A Downbeat magazine critic wrote that she is "one of those players who sounds like she was never a beginner."

fairly closely and doesn't usually do on-the-spot sit-ins) agreed. Jin grabbed her horn and started playing.

"It was like a hurricane," D'earth recalls. "She's a Cannonball player, like, Cannonball Adderly. There were people there that night who remember that. I mean, the women there who like our music, who hang out, were like, 'she is just cutting everybody a new asshole on that bandstand!'"

Jin, pleasantly surprised by the jazz she heard that night, was soon invited to join the Thursday night band. She did. "It was a blast getting to know and play with so many musicians in a small town—right away I knew I had found a new home for myself," she says. Jin, who played with the Thursday band for about a year, has since moved back to New York City. But she still thinks about those Charlottesville gigs and her music friends often.

A photo of the Thursday crew from the Jin era. Jin is pictured center, playing saxophone. Photo courtesy of Jess Martin.

That night was the perfect example of the "drama of Miller's," says D'earth, who talks about it like he still can't quite believe it happened, clapping his hand to the side of his head and exclaiming "my GOD," over and over.

The drama is creative and there's a sense of camaraderie among the musicians. Jin's quick inclusion in the Miller's scene is an example of what's stuck out most about those nights to Richelle Claiborne: the "graciousness" of the musicians and their willingness to share their space. Dawn Thompson, for instance, would regularly invite Claiborne up on stage to share her mic. And though Thompson died in August 2017, her presence and that of other Miller's regulars who have passed, like Johnny Gilmore and LeRoi Moore, remains in the memories and the music of those still playing.

It's hard not to feel the sense of community, established over more than three decades, when you step into a show at Miller's. Gina Sobel is so inspired by the Thursday night scene that she wrote a song about it. The Mighty Fine's "Thursdays Can Be Lonely" is about "all the people who gather there on Thursday nights and the storied nature of those nights," says Sobel, who at one point traded gardening for music lessons with D'earth (who she describes as a tough but encouraging teacher). "I knew about Thursdays at Miller's before I moved to Charlottesville. It has a legendary quality to it. And those nights, you walk in and it's all the best jazz musicians on stage and in the audience. You get there and you see all your friends."

Jazz Present and Jazz Future Collide

Miller's, Sobel adds, is "the creative playground for the best players in town." And it's not just the ones who've been playing for decades. Despite its long history as a venue, the Miller's music culture (particularly that of those Thursday night gigs) looks to the future even more so than to the past, nurturing the next generation of musicians.

There's a verse in Sobel's song that goes:

> Kids at the back table, eyes wide, lost in time,
> the last gasp if they don't change their minds.
> Then the trumpet dribbles in, hero of the night.
> They're in for life. Yeah, he's measured up their minds,
>   but he's always on their side.

Here, she references the local high school kids who are almost always sitting at a back table with a round of Cokes, young jazz band players whose band directors told them they have to go hear music at Miller's on a Thursday night. "There's something so magical about that," she says, "and so heartening that this music is still alive. And more young people are coming into it, and you can see it right there."

That vision was brought into crystal clear focus in the 2010s. Terri Allard, the country and folk singer-songwriter who played Miller's in its early days, started bringing her son, Will Evans, to hear music.

Gina Sobel, a multi-instrumentalist, singer, songwriter, composer, and improviser who plays folk, funk, and just about everything in between. She performs solo as well as with a variety of groups, including Choose Your Own Adventure, The Mighty Fine, and Minnush, a modern Sephardic music quartet.

Evans, who was about 12 or 13 at the time, had grown up in a musical family. But instead of following his mom's path to country and folk, he was drawn to jazz and became something of a trumpet prodigy. By the time Evans was in high school, he was taking lessons with D'earth and sitting in on some of those Thursday night gigs.

Allard treasures a photograph that Marty Phillips of the Charlottesville Jazz Society snapped of Evans and D'earth one Thursday night, the red "Miller's" sign glowing in the window behind them. Evans grins while holding his trumpet to his lips, while D'earth, also grinning, leans in and whispers in Evans' ear. Upon seeing the photo, Allard thought Evans' expression was one of adoration for D'earth. But when she mentioned this to Evans, she says the young trumpet player assured his mother that wasn't the whole story.

Evans was still in high school at the time and looked younger than his age. Allard says D'earth was teasing him: "They're just clapping 'cause you're cute."

A young Will Evans laughing with John D'earth. Photograph by Martin Phillips, www.martinphillipsart.com.

Terri Allard, a singer-songwriter born in Barboursville, Virginia, to a musical family. She hosts a long-running culture television show for the local PBS channel and has co-written a song with Mary Chapin Carpenter.

26

But D'earth remembers the night differently. Will admittedly didn't love the over-the-top clapping he sometimes got when performing: "That's what Will didn't like! He'd get really upset about it," Allard says. That aversion to excess attention is what D'earth says is actually behind Phillips' photo.

Will did indeed get extra attention that night, says D'earth. He remembers Will's frustration: "they're only doing it because I'm little and cute," Will thought. In the photo, D'earth says, he's comforting Will, telling him to pay no mind and keep on playing—they'll clap because he's *good*. What Phillips captured in the trumpeters' aside, then, is the passing of wisdom, an example of the future of jazz as cultivated at Miller's.

Evans went on to study music in New York City, but plays around Virginia with his band, Angelica X, whenever he's home. He plays at Miller's whenever he can, as those who get their start there often do. As the musicians will tell you, there's probably not another neighborhood bar with music of that caliber for hundreds, maybe thousands, of miles.

John D'earth and Will Evans playing dual trumpet at Miller's. Photograph by Martin Phillips, www.martinphillipsart.com.

After all, for D'earth, who moved here from New York City and stayed for the music and the community around it, Miller's is the place where a musician can do what they want and have all the creative freedom an artist could ask for—something that he's sure would have been entirely, or at least nearly, impossible elsewhere.

"We'll really ruin your life up there on that stage," D'earth says through laughter, because artists will search far and wide to discover that there's no place like Miller's.

FELLINI'S

Fellini's, a longtime staple of Charlottesville music and dining, opened just a few years before Miller's. As a venue and restaurant, it's gone through several eras, but its early influence on Charlottesville's downtown entertainment scene (especially the jazz scene) is undeniable. Through all of its eras, Fellini's warmly welcomed local musicians, who describe it as an intimate, comfortable space that they're always eager to play.

At the time of writing, Fellini's remained open for business. Though the restaurant has since closed, this chapter remains in present tense to preserve the wording and voice of those quoted.

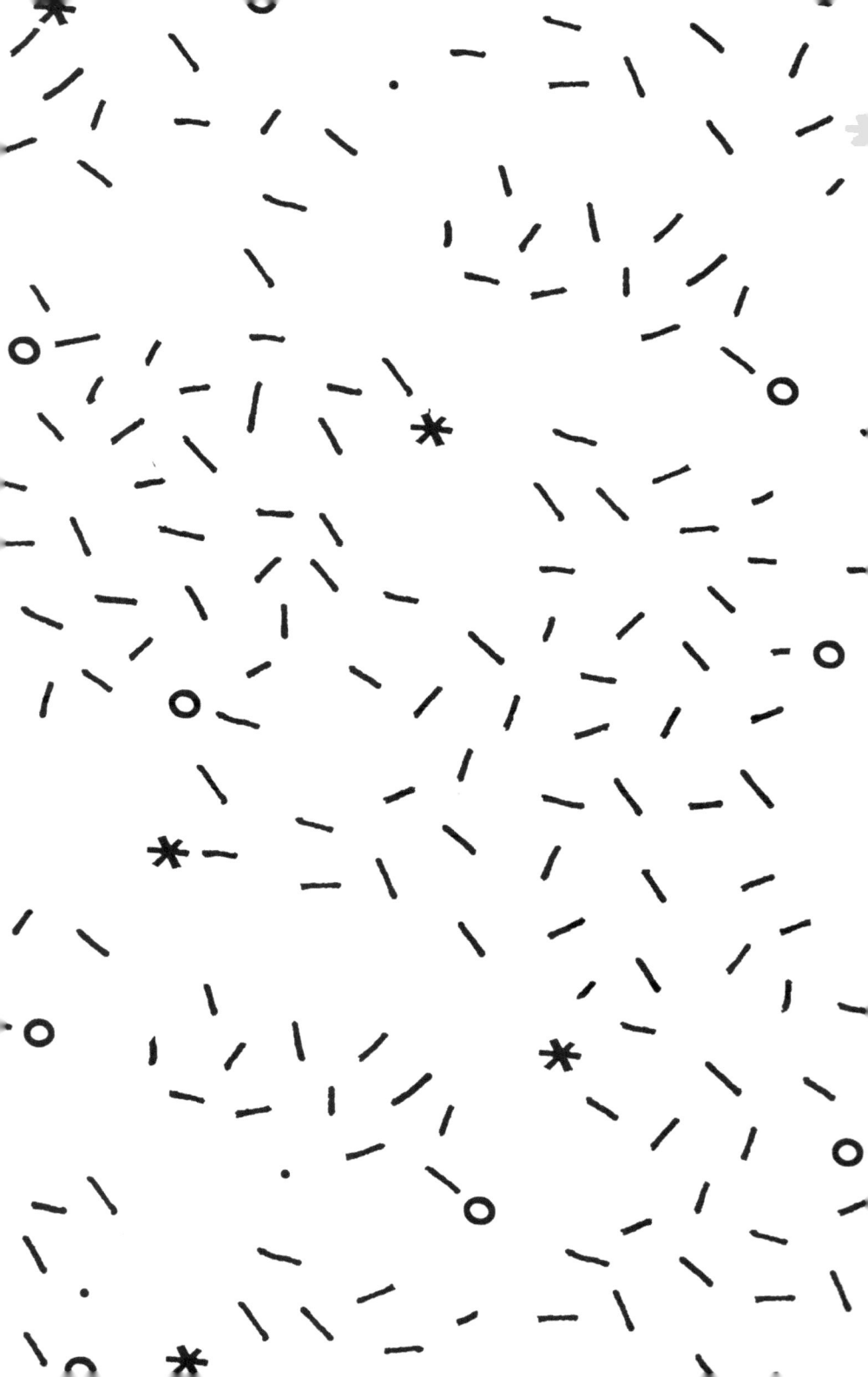

"It Feels Like Home"

An Homage to Fellini's No. 9

Fellini's No. 9 opened in October 1979 in a white stucco building on the corner of Market Street and Second Street NE. Its name is an homage to Italian film director Federico Fellini and his influential 1963 film *8 ½*, a surrealist dramatic comedy about a filmmaker struggling with his latest project.

Its owners were F. Guthrie "Chief" Gordon and Ann Porotti, the couple that opened the nearby arthouse, Vinegar Hill Theatre, just a few years earlier, on Valentine's Day 1976.[†] When Gordon and Porotti split in 1980, he got the restaurant and she got the theater.

Fellini's has a long, storied, and for a time, sordid, history. Senlin Means, who wrote under the byline J. Tobias Beard, details much of it in "The (Mostly True) Story of Fellini's," a two-part feature story that ran in C-VILLE Weekly in late September and early October of 2011. Most of the story focuses on Chief Gordon, a charming actor-turned-lawyer-turned-restaurant owner and maître-d who had a host of catchphrases and taglines, including "never admit to a fact, never deny a rumor."

> VINEGAR HILL THEATRE –
>
> Ann Porotti and F. Guthrie "Chief" Gordon opened this arthouse film theater at 220 W. Market Street on February 14–Valentine's Day–1976. It showed classic American and foreign films until it closed in 2013. A few years later, the theatre reopened to host some events for the Virginia Film Festival. Now, it's home to Light House Studio, where young people create original films.

Gordon encouraged, generously facilitated, and participated in (usually, but not always, after-hours) Bacchanalian revelry at Fellini's, all to his eventual detriment. Gordon (who simultaneously practiced personal injury law and ran the restaurant) owed the IRS for unpaid taxes on the restaurant, lost his license permanently after a string of

DUIs, and eventually pleaded guilty in June 1993 to two charges of felony embezzlement after swiping his law clients' settlement money for his own personal use.

After Gordon's legal troubles, his second wife, Trisha, ended up with the restaurant. She sold it—both the building and the business—in 1994 for $165,000 (not nearly enough to cover all the back taxes).

Whatever the true details of the restaurant's earliest days are, one subplot in the story is undeniable: Fellini's and its laid-back atmosphere shaped downtown Charlottesville as an entertainment destination.

"Before Fellini's, there wasn't much happening down there on the newly bricked-over Main Street," Means writes. "If you lived here in the '60s and you wanted to have a good time at night, then you were probably a UVA student and you probably went to The Corner. It was only in the late '70s that downtown started to become a place to go, an entertainment destination. Fellini's made it happen. Of course there were (and still are) the C&O, Court Square Tavern, and Miller's. And there was Eastern Standard and Random Row and Muldowney's, etcetera, etcetera, amen.[†] But it was Fellini's that breathed life into the scene, or tossed the lit torch on the pyre, or whatever mythic metaphor you want to use. Make no mistake, we are dealing here with the stuff of myth. The Birth of Charlottesville Cool, perhaps, or maybe the loss of its innocence, because the town has never been the same since."

EASTERN STANDARD / ESCAFE –
Located at 227 W. Main Street on the Downtown Mall, where the Whiskey Jar restaurant is today, Eastern Standard opened sometime before 1992. Around 10:00PM, it switched from bistro to gay bar (getting a liquor license for a known gay bar wasn't easy then, former owner Sean Concannon told C-VILLE Weekly in 2018, as the Virginia governor at the time was a vocal opponent of gay rights). It became Escafe in 2005. As Escafe, it continued Eastern Standard's legacy as a safe place for the queer community, even those under 21 years of age. It moved to 215 Water St. in 2012, and hosted its last meal and dance night in 2018, when the building—which also included the Ante Room and a skating rink—was purchased and razed to make room for CODE.

RANDOM ROW BOOKS –
A bookshop that also held rock, folk, hip-hop, and art shows. The building was demolished to build a hotel. For more, see volume 1.

MULDOWNEY'S PUB –
A lesbian bar on Water Street. Lackey Die, Charlottesville's first hardcore punk band, played its first show ("Slam or Scram," the flier said) there in 1983. For a while, it was the only place in town that welcomed punk music.

That part of the story, at least, is definitely true. No one would deny Fellini's influence on Charlottesville's music scene.

After Trisha Gordon sold the restaurant, it sat empty for about a decade until Jacie Dunkle revived it, welcoming back many of the restaurant's regulars, from the bohemian artists and professors to well-to-do doctors and lawyers. Dunkle also booked local musicians most nights of the week, something that continued when she sold the restaurant in 2015, bought it back in 2016, and then sold it once again to Chris and Sarah Humphreys.

Fellini's is no longer known for extraordinary debauchery (though stories about people having sex on "The Slab" and free-flowing booze persist). Yet the ghost of its past rather kindly haunts its present. The restaurant's reputation has become one of a meaningful neighborhood gathering place, one that's warm and fun and (usually due to the music) still slightly raucous on occasion.

Dick Orange sings to Jacie Dunkle. Dunkle, who revived Fellini's after the Gordon era, is pictured on the left. Dunkle also founded and owned Tin Whistle Irish Pub.
Photo courtesy of Susanna Rosen.

An Intimate Room

When Gina Sobel finishes playing a gig at one of downtown Charlottesville's various restaurant-bars or music venues, she sometimes has to carefully plan her walk back to her car. It's not for safety reasons, though.

It's because she might end up at Fellini's.

Anyone walking by the restaurant at the busy intersection of Second Street NE and Market Street is easily seduced by the soft light shining through the pane glass and by the sounds of clinking glasses, tinkling piano or wailing jazz, and deep laughter wafting through the windows and the door as it swings open and shuts behind those who couldn't resist stopping in.

"Your friends are playing, you have your instrument on your back, you go in, you play some tunes. It's just so easy," Sobel says. There's the music, the on-tap prosecco, and then, all of a sudden, it's two or two thirty in the morning, long past her self-imposed curfew.

"How do you not go in?," she asks, laughing. "You have to walk a different way if you want to get home and not stop at Fellini's."

The Bob Bennetta Trio plays the Fellini's Holiday Party in 2016.
Photograph by Martin Phillips, www.martinphillipsart.com.

Sobel's not the only local musician to experience this phenomenon. Some, like Sobel, stop in after playing their own sets. Others pop by for a nightcap after seeing a movie at The Paramount Theater or having dinner for "just a couple songs." Most end up staying and listening to their friends play music long after last call.

Fellini's lures musicians through the door like a siren calls sailors to crash on an island's rocky shore (though the collisions that happen at Fellini's are decidedly softer and much more fun).

"That's the late-night, had a few too many, go listen to Chickenhead [Blues Band]," play upbeat boogie-woogie and rhythm and blues place says Brennan Gilmore. "It's one of the more comfortable, laid-back, and celebratory venues in town. It's very informal." He refers to the way the band packs snugly into the corner of the bar room, right by the windows and on the floor rather than up on a stage. "It's this communal sense of entertainment, and a sort of equity between performer and audience. […] If you're a performer, you're amongst the crowd, and when the energy's good, and they're really going, there's no separation between performer and audience, which is cool."

Performers have to be in the right mood for this kind of show, says Gilmore, who plays mostly bluegrass and newgrass music. "If you're a grumpy artist who doesn't want people spilling beer on your amps, that's not the right place to play. But if you don't mind a nice stout stain across your Tolex, then [Fellini's is] the right joint."

"What I love about Fellini's is it's a neighborhood bar," says Terri Allard. As pricey craft cocktail bars and craft breweries have popped up in just about every neighborhood in town, the prevalence of the neighborhood bar has waned. Just a few, including Fellini's, Miller's, and Durty Nelly's over on Jefferson Park Avenue, remain.[†] "You never know who you're going to see in there," adds Allard. At Fellini's, it's impossible to know who's going to come through the door at any given time on any given night, but it's a safe bet that at least some of the faces will be familiar.

> DURTY NELLY'S –
> Located at 2200 Jefferson Park Avenue at the cusp of the Fry's Spring and JPA neighborhoods, Durty Nelly's is a bar and sandwich shop attached to a convenience store, complete with wood paneling and a working fireplace. It's hosted local music regularly since it opened in the 1970s, particularly folk and Americana. But after a change in ownership in 2021, Durty Nelly's now hosts rock acts, Irish sessions with the Blue Ridge Irish Music School, and karaoke nights, too.

A live show at Fellini's, the crowd out of view behind and to the right of the camera. Photo by Tristan Williams, courtesy of Gina Sobel.

"Anything goes" at Fellini's, says Susanna Rosen, a singer who's played the spot frequently for more than a decade with both her New Orleans-style jazz group Zuzu's Hot Five and her Cajun-folk band Bayou Faux Pas. "If you ask the audience to do a conga line, they'll do it."

And they'll do it in a tight space.

As Gilmore points out, there's no separation of patron and performer at Fellini's. Bands play tucked into the corner of the barroom, next to the pane glass windows that open onto the busy sidewalk, mere feet away from both the front door entrance and the massive wooden u-shaped bar that extends all the way to the back wall. Whatever music's happening in that room drifts into the restaurant's dining room, separated from the barroom by nothing more than an open doorway.

Racks of glassware and liquor bottles reflect soft light from pendant lamps that

Susanna Rosen, a singer and ukulele player who performs in a few different groups, including Zuzu's Hot 5 and Bayou Faux Pas. Cajun music captured her heart on a trip to New Orleans in the 1990s and hasn't left her since.

hang above the bar. At night, the room—which has wood floors, wood ceilings, and wood-paneled walls—is so dimly lit, bands usually turn on a small table lamp on the windowsill behind them so they can see their instruments, music, and one another.

All that wood—and the low ceilings—make for some stellar acoustics. "Fellini's is one of the best-sounding rooms, acoustically, that I've ever played in," says Charles Owens, who has played Fellini's often. "The combination of that corner, with the wood and the glass, it's the right amount of reflection and the right amount of absorption to really make the band sonically pleasing."

Acme Swing Mfg. Co performing at Fellini's in 2009. Susanna Rosen toured with the band, which played '30s era swing music. Photograph by Martin Phillips, www.martinphillipsart.com.

Plus, there's a real piano in the room (a rarity here in town) and that makes all the acoustic difference for jazz groups. "You can't go wrong with a bar that has a resident piano," says Susanna. "It's ready to be played. It suggests music even when there's nobody sitting at it. It's going to happen."

And it does happen, even when there's no show scheduled. While working as a host at Hamiltons at First & Main on the Downtown Mall a few years back, Sobel overheard a busker playing early Bob Dylan songs while she filled water glasses on the patio. "He looked like baby Dylan," too, she says. "I kept getting distracted from paying attention to what I was supposed to be doing, because I was listening to him. So I went and talked to him after my shift, and we ended up jamming a lot over a few days. It turned out he was just some kid traveling—like, he was doing the early Dylan thing of being a vagabond, going from city to city and sleeping on people's couches and trying to figure out the world. We played a lot together for the couple days that he was in Charlottesville, and we were talking about this one Dylan song that's on piano." Remembering the piano at Fellini's, just up the block from where they were jamming on the Mall, Sobel dashed him up there on a whim to play the Dylan song. Dunkle owned the restaurant at the time and Sobel says she welcomed the impromptu jam session, bringing each of the young musicians a plate of spaghetti and sauce to eat.

Paul Rosen, who plays with Susanna in Zuzu's Hot Five and Bayou Faux Pas, as well as in Cajun-punk band Jolie Fille, says that playing so close to such a big bar can be a bit physically and musically awkward. "But on the other hand, it's an advantage. If you have ten people there dancing, and they're dancing right in front of you, it feels full. But then, you can have another 20 behind them just in chairs. So, [Fellini's] can feel full at ten, at 20, and then you can get even more packed in around [the bar]. You never have an empty room—or, it never feels like an empty room."

Cajun punk band Jolie Fille performing at Fellini's, complete with washboard. Paul Rosen, who's also an accomplished contra dance caller, is pictured on the right. Photo courtesy of Susanna Rosen.

And when the windows are open on a warm night, it can sometimes feel like the whole city is in the room. The pane glass windows open onto Second Street NE, one of two one-way streets that cross the Downtown Mall, and pedestrians, cars, and trolleys constantly amble by and idle at the stoplight. The sounds of car radios, pre-recorded semi-robotic bus announcements, impatient car horns, and snippets of tipsy, too-loud conversations drift in and mingle with the music.

Occasionally, cars turn the wrong way down the one way, and that's a whole other level of sonic chaos for a band (and everyone else) to deal with.

Playing next to the open windows can be an olfactory adventure for the band, too. Wafts of bus exhaust, strong perfumes, pungent colognes, cigarettes, and the occasional whiff of marijuana all enter the restaurant on the breeze, momentarily eclipsing the smell of the Fellini's kitchen.

Below: Fellini's, as seen through the window. Photo by Eze Amos.

Above: Flyer for a Jolie Fille show at Fellini's. Photo courtesy of Susanna Rosen.

Passersby tend to stop and watch the band from the sidewalk outside the window (usually unbeknownst to the band) and that can be both a wonderful and unsettling playing experience, depending on the person, the musicians say.

"One of the craziest experiences that I've had as a musician happened [at Fellini's]," says Ivan Orr. When Orr plays music, he usually focuses on what he's doing. But one night, he could feel someone's presence, a pair of eyes watching him, though he couldn't see anyone. When the band finished the song (he doesn't remember what they were playing, but it was probably something funky and soulful), a woman behind him laughed in delight before saying something to the effect of, "I was mesmerized! I've never heard anyone play like that in person!"

"I kind of giggled," says Orr. "When you do something [regularly], you kind of take it for granted, like, that's what we do." He wonders if her response had something to do with the fact that this band was playing a kind of music—Black music—that isn't often given a stage in Charlottesville, but that gets occasional space at Fellini's.[†]

FELLINI'S & VINEGAR HILL

More on this in a forthcoming volume about the Jefferson School African American Heritage Center. But, it is important to note here that Fellini's is located on the cusp of Vinegar Hill, a once thriving majority Black neighborhood near what is now downtown Charlottesville. It was full of homes, churches, shops, a grocery store, and more, that the city demolished in the mid-1960s for an "urban renewal project." Because of this and other factors, many Black residents say they've been made to feel unwelcome in downtown Charlottesville.

"What's been cool about [Fellini's] is, for the most part, the acceptance," he says. Orr grew up in town playing music with Chief Gordon and Ann Porotti's son, Ian (their first bar gig was at Miller's). He's played a variety of gigs at Fellini's, from occasional sets with singer Richelle Claiborne to annual tribute shows honoring the late George Melvin.[†]

Orr loves to see who shows up to Fellini's gigs. It's usually a curious cross-section of people, he says, "dyed-in-the-wool Charlottesville people, people we went to high school with, people from the neighborhood,

GEORGE MELVIN –

A homegrown Hammond B-3 organ legend who shared a stage with mega stars like Al Hirt, Miles Davis, Aretha Franklin, Nancy Wilson, Johnny Cash, Charlie Daniels, Ray Charles, Teddy Pendergrass, and others.

The late organ legend George Melvin at Fellini's in 2008. Photograph by Martin Phillips, www.martinphillipsart.com.

and then Fellini's regulars. And the odd person walking down Second Street," he adds, laughing.

The atmosphere inside Fellini's shifts with the sun. During the day it's a great place to have, say, a Mother's Day brunch, according to singer Richelle Claiborne: she did exactly that a few years ago with her mother, aunts, and some friends. (She recommends the beignets and the bloody mary bar.)

Paul Rosen says one of the strangest parts of playing a daytime set is what he calls the "bus eclipse." The Fellini's windows are so close to the street that when a bus whizzes by—which is every 15 minutes or so—it blocks out all the light for a second or two. It's not so much bothersome as it is curious, a quirk unique to Fellini's.

But when the sun goes down, Fellini's adopts more of a jazz lounge vibe. It becomes a place where "you feel like you can let loose and have fun, without being judged," Claiborne says while raising an eyebrow, speaking as if she knows from experience. She's pretty sure Fellini's is the only place in town, or one of the only places, where one can get a Peroni beer. She loves that it's right next door to the Elks Lodge, a fraternal organization, which sometimes brings a completely different clientele through the door (they'll share smokes with Fellini's folks and then come in for a drink … or two).[†] "It's a great place for me to work out new material. It's a great place for me to get new fans because, with the windows open, people walk by and they're like, 'I want to go in *there.*' Every memory of performing there has been a good one."

That's the thing about Fellini's. When musicians talk about playing and hearing music at Fellini's, for the most part, they don't talk about specific shows. They talk about what it *feels* like. It feels "classic," "intimate," and "warm." It "feels like home." They talk about how much they love to play there.

A Fond Farewell

But some sets stand out. Particularly, the one pianist Hod O'Brien played before he died in November 2016.

O'Brien was active in the New York City jazz scene in the 1950s. His career took off after playing piano on Donald Byrd, Art Farmer, and Idrees Sulieman's 1957 record *Three Trumpets.* Though he was primarily known as a bebop pianist, he could play a variety of styles and accompanied such artists as Archie Shepp, Sheila Jordan, Chet Baker, and Sonny Greer (who himself drummed for Duke Ellington).

O'Brien also taught music at UVA for years, and performed often at Fellini's with his wife, jazz singer Stephanie Nakasian, and their daughter, Veronica Swift, also a jazz singer.

Toward the end of O'Brien's battle with cancer, Jacie Dunkle called him and Nakasian: "We want to hear Hod perform one last time. Would he do it?" Nakasian remembers O'Brien had no energy, but he agreed. That night, he sat at the piano and played a couple tunes, then went outside to rest in Dunkle's truck, parked nearby, before coming back in to play two more, then going back outside to rest.

Nakasian, who prefers to socialize rather than sing at Fellini's, says she's had "amazing social moments" at Fellini's, but Hod's last-ever performance tops the list.

"That was a sweet night," agrees Allard. One that really could only happen, and happen in that particular way, at Fellini's. "Fellini's has that feel. It has that potential, to be that special place where people gather [for] camaraderie, and the sense of family."

Fellini's even draws listeners on snowy nights, notes Gary Funston. Charlottesvillians typically don't leave the house when there's even the possibility of a snowflake falling from the sky, but no matter the weather, it "seems like all the jazz-lovers in town have made their way to Fellini's." It may be a small crowd, but it's an audience nonetheless.

Perhaps that's because Fellini's is one of the few remaining spots in town that regularly hosts jazz. Years ago, there were more venues for it: Escafe (closed in 2018, its building demolished within a year), Bon (a hippie tea room that vacated its spot in the pink warehouse on South St. in 2015), Tin Whistle (closed after Near Year's Eve 2019).[†] "You could walk to all of them," Funston notes. The downtown Charlottesville jazz scene was "a pretty happening place. But not anymore."

The other regularly reliable downtown spot for jazz is, of course, Miller's, which has its own storied history and unique identity. Those who are unfamiliar with both spots shouldn't conflate the two.

Fellini's is "so much more subdued" than Miller's, says Pete Spaar, who, in addition to Miller's Thursday nights, has played at Fellini's the first Saturday of every month for at least a decade. "You couldn't get a crowd as much as you do [at] Miller's because it's off the main drag. But I prefer to play [Fellini's] because they have that piano, a very nice piano, in that space. […] To a jazz group, to have a real acoustic piano, even though it's an upright, makes a world of difference to the type of music we want to play," he says.

That both Fellini's and Miller's can exist (in the same city block, no less) is a testament not just to the wealth of musical talent in the area, but to people's appetite for it.

TIN WHISTLE IRISH PUB –

Jacie Dunkle opened Tin Whistle at 609 East Market Street in 2014. The pub served Irish food and beer and hosted regular Irish music sessions. It closed at midnight on Dec. 31, 2019, mere weeks before the COVID-19 pandemic hit.

BON –

BON opened around 2009 and first existed in the York Place shopping center on Water Street before moving to the first floor of the pink warehouse on 100 W. South Street. It was a cafe that hosted art shows, poetry slams, and music, including jazz and folk concerts as well as a Saturday morning drum circle. It closed sometime in the 2010s.

Most bar and restaurant music gigs in town come with a complimentary meal and a few drinks. But at the end of the night, unless there's a cover charge, those gigs usually don't pay much (especially when a fee is divided among band members) and bands often rely on tips to take home or put into the band fund.

But at Fellini's, people are more apt to show their appreciation that way. Fellini's customers, according to Susanna Rosen, "notice the tip jar and appreciate the band in a way that they don't at other places. So, if you put that crystal bowl on the piano, or on the bar close to the band, people will appreciate, pause, tip, nod at you as they go out. They look you in the eye, and you realize they've had a good experience."

Closing

Dunkle sold Fellini's #9 to longtime locals Chris and Sarah Humphrey in August 2017. The couple kept the spirit of the place going, but soon faced extraordinary challenges that they couldn't overcome, even with the love and support from its customers.

Sarah died in August 2019, and the COVID-19 pandemic hit just months later, putting enormous strain on the restaurant and music industries. Starting in March 2020, restaurants shut down for months. Fellini's served

Bob Bennetta at Fellini's. Photo by Eze Amos.

takeout and delivery, and tried to have outdoor seating on the sidewalk outside the restaurant, but Chris said the city turned them down.

The restaurant did not receive any grant or loan assistance, unlike other businesses locally and across the country. It opened for dining service, with windows open, music going, and COVID precautions in place, in July 2020.

But that wasn't enough. "WE TRIED EVERYTHING," the restaurant wrote in a Facebook post announcing its closing.

Hundreds of people wrote back, expressing thanks, gratitude, and sadness.

Fellini's closed after a sold-out dinner service on December 19, 2020. "We say goodbye to the end of an epic staple in the community," Humphrey wrote in a post on the restaurant's Facebook page. "We are devastated and heartbroken just like you."

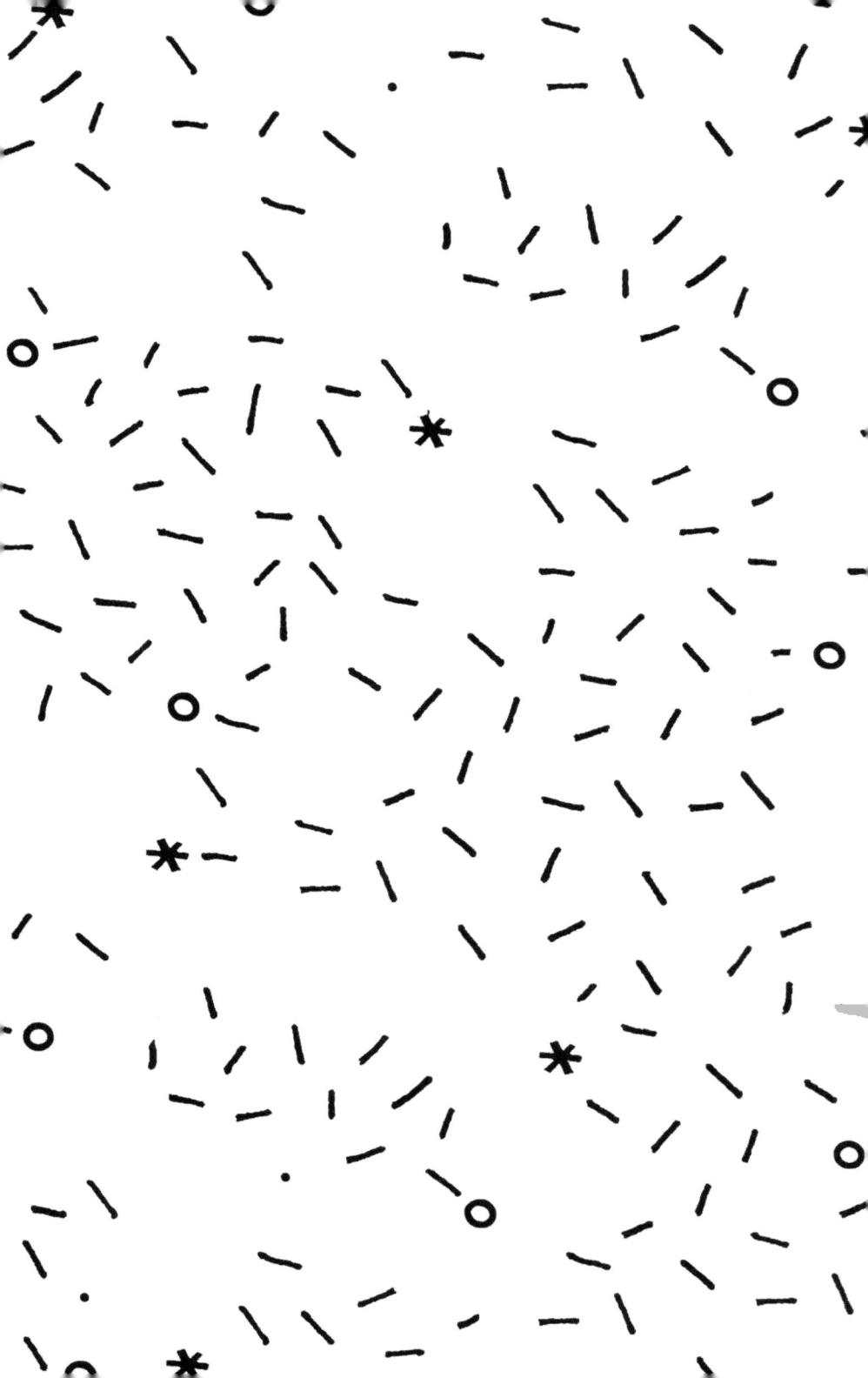

Bonus Tracks

Remembering Legendary Shows at The Mineshaft and Blue Moon Diner

The web of Charlottesville music is always being undone and re-spun, with places closing and opening, or starting and stopping support for local music. Scenes evolve as venues change hands, booking agents leave town, bands break up, venues close, and new groups arise to fill voids left by former pillars of the music community.

Venues both large and small, remembered and forgotten, intertwine in the history of music in Charlottesville. Some, like Miller's, remain bastions of the music scene today. Some, like Fellini's have shuttered their doors, inviting others to pick up where they left off.

But Miller's and Fellini's never stood alone. Other venues, like The Mineshaft and Blue Moon Diner, helped nourish the same scenes, hosting local acts like Plutonium and bringing in monumental artists like Sun Ra. While we couldn't devote as much space to these venues, they helped Charlottesville's music culture evolve right alongside Miller's and Fellini's.

While The Mineshaft has been closed for years, Blue Moon Diner remains a thriving community hub, continuing to regularly host live music events.

With Charlottesville constantly evolving, it remains to be seen what venues and groups will add to the history of Fellini's and The Mineshaft, joining venues like Miller's and Blue Moon in keeping Charlottesville music alive.

The Mineshaft

*The Mineshaft operated at 1106-1107 West Main Street, just
past The Corner from about 1975 to late 1989. When The Mine-
shaft was in operation, you could walk down the street from The
Corner to downtown and hear music drifting from it's windows,
alongside music from Zipper's bar and Traxx nightclub (where
Dave Matthews Band frequently played in its early years). The
Mineshaft hosted some iconic acts over the years: in addition to
The Sun Ra Arkestra, Muddy Waters also played there.*

Sun Ra at The Mineshaft. Photo by Chuck Taylor

*The building is currently home to The Draftsman, a hotel owned
by Marriott, the largest hotel chain in the world, and The Ridley,
a restaurant for Southern cuisine.*

Sun Ra at The Mineshaft

Told by Matthew Simon, longtime WTJU DJ "Rocker Panels." Simon co-hosts the weekly radio show "Carry the Zero" on Thursdays from 2:00-4:00 PM with fellow WTJU DJs Stevik and Lady D.

This dude from WTJU came and spoke at my concert band class in high school. He was talking about all these shows that were coming up and [we should] "buy this [concert] pass, it's cheaper for students." And me, being in high school, I didn't even think he meant UVA students. I thought he meant high school students. So, all of these shows are at Cabell Hall [at UVA] and this and that.

[But he was like], "oh yeah, there's this [other] show, but I don't know if you guys are gonna be able to go because you're not 18, but maybe we can try to get you guys in. It's at the Mineshaft." And that's when me and my friend were like, "we should try to get this pass, because we want to go to the Mineshaft!" So, we go. We don't even know what the hell we're going to see.

We were like, trumpet players in this [high school] jazz band, but our jazz teacher at the time was teaching us like, Dick Clark Live kind of stuff. Like, "Up, Up, and Away, My Beautiful Balloon" jazz music. And we go to this jazz show at the Mineshaft and it's Sun Ra? It was the most incredible thing I have ever seen. Changed my life. Because we were under 18, not only did we have X's on our hands, we had to stand in this little roped-off area to be separated from everyone else. And I guess they maybe allowed us [in] because there were like, these other children running around who were with the band? I don't know. I remember me and my other friend who played trumpet and my other friend who played oboe in a concert band at Charlottesville High School, went and saw Sun Ra at the Mineshaft. Just because we wanted to go see a show. How cool is that?

All the other shows were at Cabell Hall. There were all these old people there, and I remember it was that kind of thing where it'd be a jazz player and a … drummer, a vibraphone, a guitar, and like, a bassist, and it would be a 20-minute vibes solo and you're like, "what time are my parents coming to pick me up? Jesus." But that Sun Ra show (in October 1989) was like my first-ever concert, small concert. I'd seen Iron Maiden at Hampton Coliseum or something beforehand, but never something like Sun Ra, which I was a little confused by. It was definitely way over my head, but you'll never forget the robes, and all the people.

Blue Moon Diner

Blue Moon Diner, located at 606 West Main Street, opened in 1979 (previously that space had been a restaurant called the Waffle House—not part of the national franchise—that opened in 1949). The funky, old-school diner with band stickers all over the place, crates of LPs in the windows, and a sideways Elvis bust near the turntable behind the counter, regularly hosts local music, and for a while, hosted Charlottesville Lady Arm Wrestling (CLAW) in its back parking lot. Parking lot gigs ended, though, when a wealthy developer put a fancy six-story apartment building directly behind (and over) the diner.

Above: advertising wall for Blue Moon Diner events and offerings.

Above: Exterior Sign of Blue Moon Diner.

Plutonium at Blue Moon Diner

Told by Matthew Simon, longtime WTJU DJ "Rocker Panels." Simon co-hosts the weekly radio show "Carry the Zero" on Thursdays from 2:00–4:00 PM with fellow WTJU DJs Stevik and Lady D.

My buddy and I went to see Warren Zevon at Crossroads—it was like a Wednesday night (August 30, 1995) or something. "Fuck it, let's go see Warren Zevon." We got there at 10 o'clock and it was over. We were like, "fuck this place," and we went to Blue Moon Diner because we knew Plutonium [was playing]—Matthew Willner, Houston Ross, and Johnny Gilmore on drums.

That night, Johnny Gilmore wasn't playing. But this guy Skinny Brown was playing, like, a 250-pound African American dude with an afro [word is that Skinny Brown played drums with James Brown back in the day].[†] And those guys were just laying it down. They used to do this funk thing all the time. They would play everywhere in Charlottesville.

To see them at the diner was actually kind of a weird thing. I don't think I'd ever seen them there before. And there were like 10, 15 other people there. The most diverse crowd I'd ever seen, ever. There were some, like, redneck dudes, some ladies hanging out. I don't know where they came from at all. And there was this skinny Black dude behind the bar along with the regular sort of Rosie the Riveter [server]. These guys were just playing funk music and having a good time with everyone in the place, and it's so tight, you know? It was hot and it was summer and I remember every single detail. Everyone was drinking those Sam Adams honey brown drinks, [which were] gross, but that's what everyone was into back then, [the ones] with the green label. [...] Skinny Brown [...] was so big [...] he kept pushing the bass drum forward and he would have to do this thing where he hit the high hat or the crash cymbal and he'd have to pull the drums back to him because he just kept inching up forward. I don't know why it was like that. We just spontaneously went there and had the best time. Screw Warren Zevon. We have the best shit here, right now.

> BERNARD C. "SKINNY" BROWN — A Charlottesville born-and-raised drummer who played with the Gospel Four, among other groups. He was rumored to have played with the Godfather of Soul, James Brown. He died in 2007.

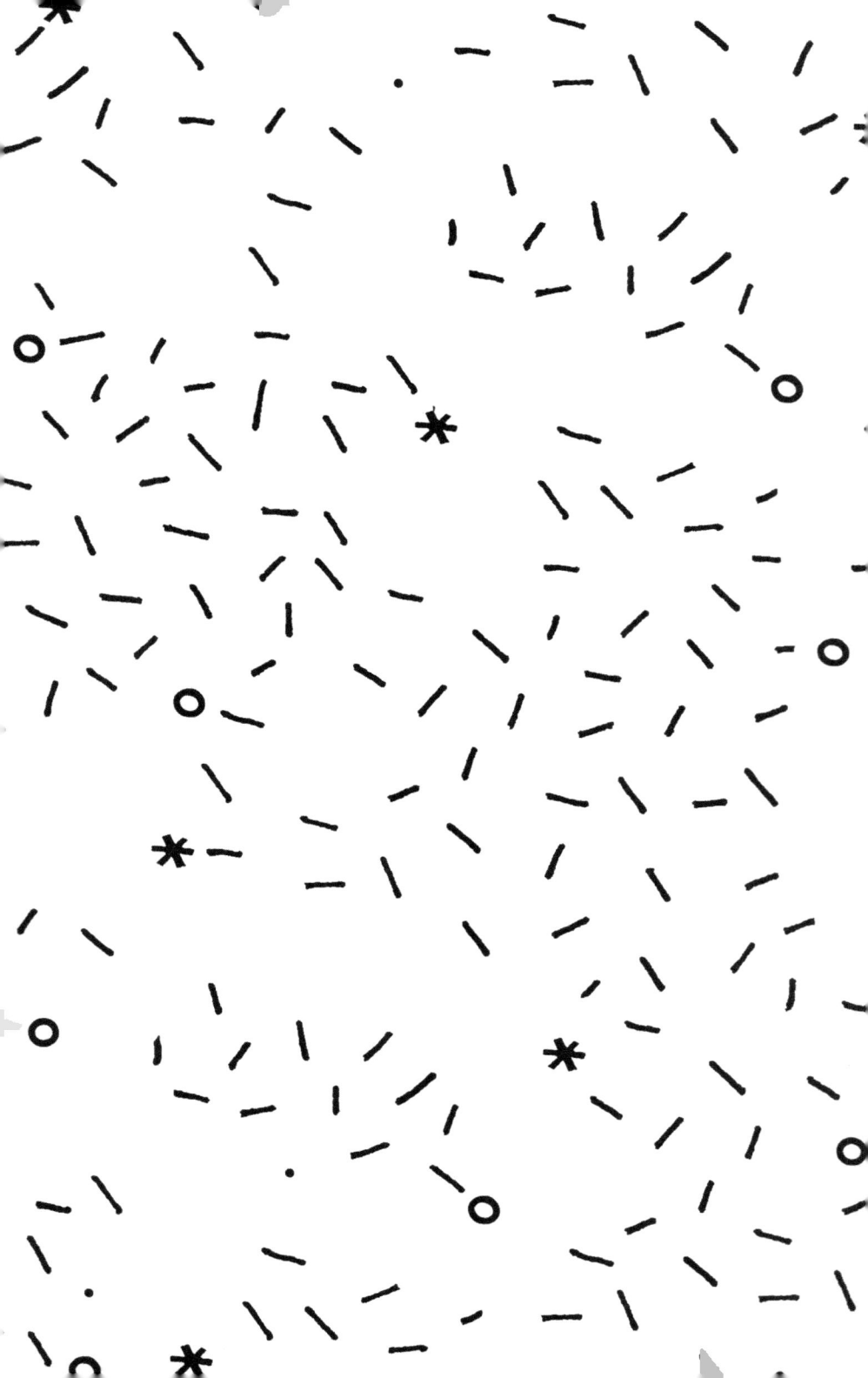

Acknowledgements

For their contributions to the Charlottesville music scene and to the author during the researching, interviewing, and writing process for this volume, a very loud and warm thanks to:

Davis Salisbury

Sophia Moore

Terri Allard

Eze Amos

Richelle Claiborne

John D'earth

Jeff Decker

Jeyon Falsini

Gary Funston

Brennan Gilmore

Dhara Goradia

Corey Harris

Pureum Jin

Jess Martin

Senlin Means

Jamal Millner

Cathy Monnes

Stephanie Nakasian

Ivan Orr

Charles Owens

Martin Phillips

Jay Pun

Susanna Rosen

Paul Rosen

Mike Rosensky

Leslie Scott-Jones

Matthew Simon

Gina Sobel

Pete Spaar

Steve Tharp

Sarah White

Special Thanks

This project would not have been possible without the generous funding of WTJU, the University of Virginia, and Virginia Humanities. Our especial gratitude to WTJU Radio, the UVA Vice Provost for the Arts, UVA Arts Council, and Virginia Humanities.

This project is also indebted to the work of two illustrious artists. The portraits that appear throughout are the work of Sarah Everton, whose work can be found at sarah-everton.com.

The cover art was created by printer, illustrator, and Charlottesville musician Thomas Dean. Below is an image of one of many of Thomas's bands, Order—previously Order of the Dying Orchid—performing at Twisted Branch Tea Bazaar, the first venue featured in this series.

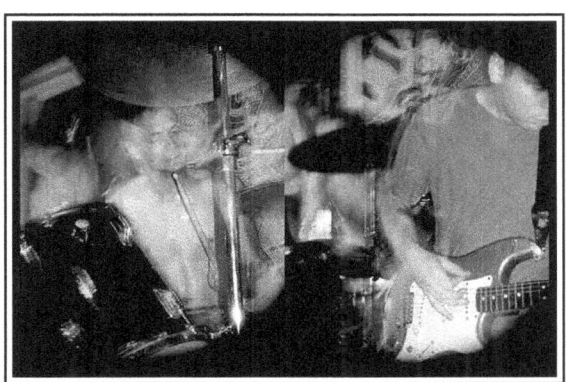

About the Author

Erin O'Hare is a local journalist, musician, and DJ, co-hosting *Ye Olde Tuesday Afternoon Rocke Show* and *Black Circle Revolution* on WTJU 91.1 FM/wtju.net. She also books music at Visible Records, a community art studio and gallery space that contains an antifascist book shop. For at least 40 hours each week, she is the neighborhoods reporter for the community-focused Charlottesville Tomorrow, where she writes in-depth stories mostly about housing, specifically the ongoing housing crisis.

Erin had wanted to write a book since she started reading them when she was four. She did, and it was harder and a lot less fun than she thought. Now that book manuscript is this zine series, which was also harder, but a lot more fun, than she thought.

She lives in so-called Charlottesville, on unceded Monacan and Manahoac lands, with her partner (who she met while writing this very series), their two cats, and their out of control record collection.